WE ARE STILL HERE

NATIVE AMERICANS TODAY

A Story to Tell

Traditions of a Tlingit Community

by **Richard Nichols**

Photographs by **D. Bambi Kraus**

Lerner Publications Company ● Minneapolis

Series Editors: LeeAnne Engfer, Gordon Regguinti
Series Consultant: W. Roger Buffalohead

The photograph on page 40 is by Marge Nannauck.

Richard Nichols offers a special thank-you to Frances Nannauck Kraus for granting permission to tell her story, sharing her knowledge of Tlingit culture, and graciously providing advice. It was her paper on the Kake Indians, written when she was a 17-year-old girl, that provided the inspiration for this book.

Illustrations by Carly Bordeau

Website address: www.lernerbooks.com

LIBRARY OF CONGRESS CATALOGING-IN-PUBLICATION DATA

Nichols, Richard, 1948–
    A story to tell : traditions of a Tlingit community / by Richard Nichols ; photographs by D. Bambi Kraus.
        p. cm. — (We are still here)
    Includes bibliographical references.
    Summary: An eleven-year-old Tlingit girl travels to Kake, Alaska, where she learns about her family's heritage from stories her grandmother tells.
    ISBN 0-8225-2661-1 (lib. bdg. : alk. paper).
    1. Tlingit Indians—Juvenile literature. [1. Tlingit Indians. 2. Indians of North America—Alaska.] I. Kraus, D. Bambi, ill. II. Title. III. Series.
E99.T6N53 1998
979.8'004972—dc21   97-9592

Manufactured in the United States of America
1 2 3 4 5 6 – JR – 03 02 01 00 99 98

In honor and memory of Paul and Lottie Nannauck,
who kept the history of Kake alive

Preface

We all have stories to tell. Some people paint pictures or take photographs that tell about a special place. Some of us tell stories with written words. Other people use spoken words as a way of expressing their stories. Indian people have been telling their stories for many thousands of years.

Many of us have learned our own ways of storytelling. I am a writer. My friend Bambi Kraus is a wonderful photographer. I have always admired the photographs Bambi takes and has hanging in her home. But I had never seen any of her Alaska photographs until I saw one called "Uncle Leonard's House" at an art show. At first I thought it was a simple black-and-white photograph of a house by the sea. But as I looked at it more carefully, I realized it was much more complicated. There was a light brush of blue on the sea behind the house and a touch of faint gold in the distant sky. I could see that the house, made of large planks of wood, was very old. The wood looked like it had been cut by hand, not by machine. The photo had won a prize for best color photograph. I could see why. It told the story of a person's love for a special place. This unique photograph made me think of a memory or a dream—of a place that is faintly but always remembered, like something from childhood.

That's what good stories do—they help us remember a time from the past or teach us something new. This story is about remembering those special times and places, even if other people want you to forget them.

Bambi's mother, Frances Nannauck Kraus, was sent to boarding school as a young girl. In those days, Indian children were sent to faraway schools, usually church schools. These children were told to forget about being Indian and learn how to be "civilized Americans." They were not allowed to speak their native languages or learn about their own people. Because young Frances couldn't talk about her life as a Tlingit Indian, she wrote a paper about it. This paper was the story of a young girl remembering her culture from a distant and foreign place. Writing down this history was her way of holding her Tlingit memories close. One day, she would tell the story to people who were worthy of her trust.

Richard Nichols and D. Bambi Kraus

This book is about the ways that we Indian people regain our history. It is about our feelings for the places we live and our feelings for our children—the special people who will carry on our history. For American Indian people, education is not separate from one's own life—learning about history is the discovery of one's own self.

"Let's go for a walk," Fran said to her granddaughter, Marissa. "I have a story to tell you." It was midmorning, and they had just finished breakfast. The sun was bright, skimming across the bay to the island.

They were sitting in the house that Marissa's grandmother, Frances Nannauck Kraus, had grown up in. It was the old family home in Kake, Alaska. Kake lies on a small island off the coast of the state's southeastern panhandle and is home to many Tlingit people (pronounced KLINK-it).

"What's the story you have to tell?" asked Marissa. This was Marissa's first trip to her family's hometown of Kake. She and Grandma Fran had come for the family reunion that had taken place the day before. Marissa had met many of her relatives. She especially liked meeting her cousins who are about the same age as she is. There was lots of food to eat, some she had never eaten before. All of her relatives exchanged presents with each other. Marissa got a special bracelet from Aunt Bambi.

Marissa Charlotte Kraus is an 11-year-old Tlingit girl. Part of the time Marissa lives with her father, Harold Kraus, her stepmother, Lynn, and her stepbrother, Paka. Other times Marissa lives with her mother, Sadia. Marissa has a dog named Maggie.

Marissa and both of her parents live in Bellevue, Washington. Bellevue is a suburb of Seattle, the largest city in the state. Over two million people live in the greater Seattle area. Marissa's grandmother lives in Seattle. Fran and Marissa see each other as often as they can.

Top right: *Marissa, her father, and Maggie*

Bottom left: *Marissa and her grandmother, Frances Nannauck Kraus*

Kake is a permanent village of the Tlingit Indians. The temperature during the summer is usually in the 50s, but sometimes it reaches into the 80s.

Marissa was happy to spend a whole week with her grandmother, especially in the village of Kake. It is on Kupreanof (Koo-PREE-uh-nawf) Island, one of the traditional homelands of the Tlingit Indians. Most of the 700 people who live in Kake are Tlingit, which means "the People." Altogether, there are more than 15,000 Tlingit Indians in the United States. Most of them live in southeastern Alaska.

Along this southeastern coast are many islands covered with rain forests of cedar, spruce, fir, and hemlock. The ocean waters between the islands and the mainland are known as the Inside Passage. The waters in these areas are fairly warm and keep the island climate mild. The waters are filled with fish and shellfish. These animals provide food for seals, sea lions, and sea otters, as well as whales and porpoises. The islands are home to deer, bears, and many small mammals.

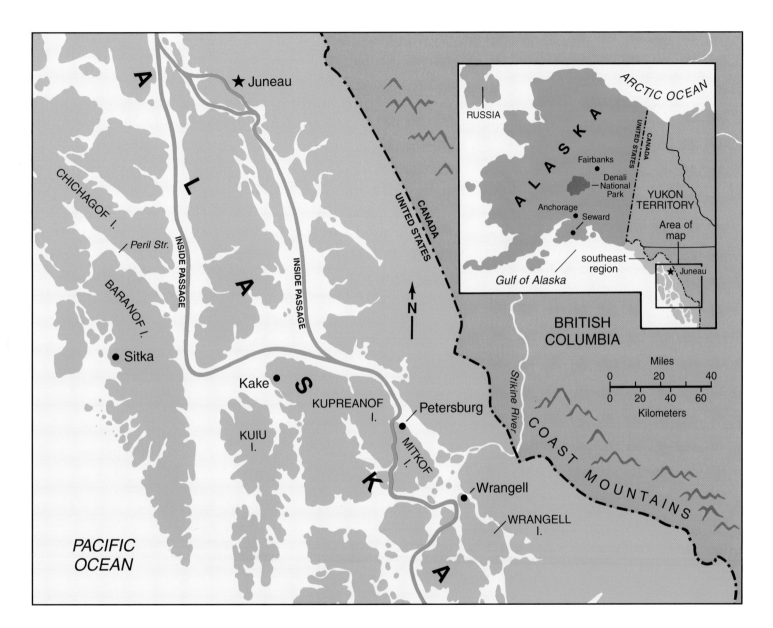

Kupreanof Island is part of Alaska's panhandle, the southeastern part of the state. The village of Kake is about 95 air miles south of Juneau, Alaska's state capital.

13

The Tlingits traditionally traded fish, game, and furs up and down the Inside Passage. They traveled from village to village in huge dugout canoes. Some of these canoes were as long as 30 feet and could hold 15 to 20 people. Seagoing canoes were even longer—up to 70 feet long.

A dugout canoe was made by hollowing out a huge, yellow cedar log. Using axes, the Tlingit men would chop a hole in one side of the log as much as they could. After that, they would build a small fire in the hole they'd created and let it burn. Then they'd put the fires out and dig out the ashes. They'd burn and dig again and again until there was enough room for people to sit in the log. By this time, the sides of the log were fairly thin. By wetting them and pressing hot stones against them, the men were able to bend the sides of the canoe out and up.

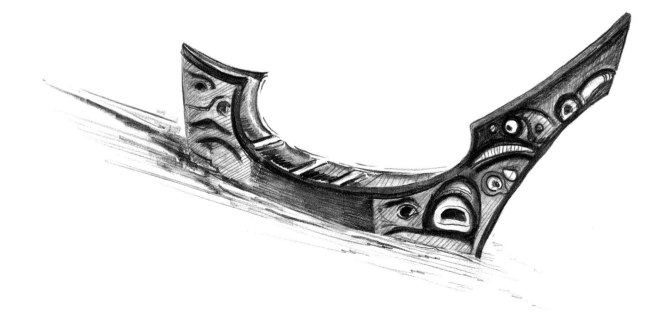

The Tlingit people of Kake are sometimes called Kake Indians. In the past, the Kake Indians were considered to be fierce and rebellious by other Tlingits and other tribes. In the early 1800s, the Kake Indians fought the efforts of Russians who tried to convert them from their traditional way of life. Later, the Kake Indians resisted American missionaries who wanted them to give up their traditional beliefs, even though the Americans burned down some Tlingit villages.

An important part of Tlingit history is about keeping native beliefs and values alive through many generations of change. Fran felt it was time for Marissa to learn more about what it means to be a Kake Indian.

This is a view of the Inside Passage from Peril Strait, between Baranof and Chichagof Islands.

On their way up the hill, Marissa and Fran could see the totem pole from the downtown float dock in Kake.

"*L*et's walk up to the totem pole," Fran said to Marissa as they started up the hill. The air was a little cool, but they knew it would warm up soon. "I've always loved coming to Kake. I'm so glad we can finally share this together."

Fran added, "You know, Marissa, there is so much to learn here about yourself and your people. The Tlingits have been on this island for thousands of years. But did you know they have not always lived here?"

"No, Grandma Fran."

"A long time ago, large sheets of ice called glaciers covered the land. During this time, the Tlingits lived on the mainland along the Stikine (Stih-KEEN) River. Our people were divided into two groups, as they are today. Some people were called Raven people and others were Eagle people. A Raven could never marry another Raven. An Eagle could not marry another Eagle. That would be like marrying your brother or sister. You see, the Creator made the Raven and Eagle peoples so they could live with each other," said Fran.

"Why did they move from where they were, Grandma?" Marissa asked.

"Well, it was very cold where they lived. The Creator told them they would find a better place to live in the West. So they walked for hundreds of miles across the mountains toward the coast. They carried as many of their clothes and other goods as they could," Fran said. "Sometimes they had to walk right under the cliff of a glacier. They could hear the tall glacier groan, as if a huge chunk of ice were going to break off any minute. It was a hard journey, but they finally made it."

Fran and Marissa stopped to catch their breath. They looked around at the beautiful trees and flowers along the path. Fran continued, "Some of the Raven and Eagle peoples settled on the coast. Others went over to the islands. That is how a small band of Raven people and Eagle people happened to set up a fishing camp that later became the town of Kake. Marissa, did you know that the way most people pronounce 'Kake' is different than the way the Tlingit people say it? Instead of saying it like the sweet cakes you like to eat, we say *Kaa'k* (KUH-ck). It means 'daybreak.'"

Grandma Fran grew up in this area of Kake, along with her sisters and brothers.

From the town of Kake, the mountains on Baranof Island can be seen.

Marissa tried to pronounce it. It wasn't easy. She said the word in her mind as she walked. All of a sudden, she heard a funny noise coming from above. It sounded like a baby gurgling "kluh-kluh, kluh-kluh."

Fran laughed. "Well, it looks like Raven heard us talking. It sounds like he is trying to talk to us," she said. "When I was a little girl, we used to listen to Raven and laugh when he made that noise. *Kluh-kluh* sounds exactly like the Tlingit word for 'man.'"

Marissa looked up. A large black bird was flying over them. Sure enough, it seemed to be talking to them. Grandma Fran talked to Raven. He answered back, and Marissa laughed.

Fran said, "See, he knows I am from the Raven people. A long time ago, our people could talk to Raven and understand what he was saying. Now we can talk back by making the sounds that Raven makes, but we don't understand what the sounds mean. We can only try to guess."

Clear streams and lush greenery are all part of southeastern Alaska's natural beauty.

After a few minutes, Fran and Marissa started walking up the hill again. Fran asked Marissa, "Do you know you are an Eagle and your father is a Raven? And that your father and I belong to the Frog clan?"

Marissa remembered that her father had told her a little bit about it. "Well, I know I am of the Eagle people, but I'm not sure what that means, Grandma. And I've never heard of the Frog clan," Marissa said.

"Well, let me see, how can I explain the Frog clan," said Fran. "Remember how I said the Creator made the Eagle and Raven peoples so they could live together? Under each kind of people, there are other divisions. These are called clans. Every Kake Indian belongs to a clan. Each clan has a name. Some of those clans are Frog, Dog Salmon, Killer Whale, Seal, Land Otter, Shark, and Bear."

21

A family friend and member of the Keex' Kwaan dance group wore the designs of a raven at the family reunion.

"At the family reunion, you met many of your relatives," Fran continued. "Remember the man and woman that people called Grandpa Kelly and Grandma Betty? They were wearing traditional Tlingit clothes with designs on them. They only wear these special clothes for important occasions. You can tell what clan they belong to by the designs on their clothes."

"What clans do Grandma Betty and Grandpa Kelly belong to?" asked Marissa.

"Well, Grandpa Kelly is from the Eagle people. He is also part of the Bear clan. So the clothes he wore had both the Eagle and Bear designs on them," said Fran. "Grandma Betty is a Raven from the Frog clan. Her clothes had those designs. She's my aunt, and she and my mother were from the Frog clan. You see, your clan comes from your mother's side, so I am from the Frog clan, too."

This was getting a little hard for Marissa to follow, but she tried to make sense of it. "So a clan is sort of like a family name, like my last name that comes from my dad's family. But in the Tlingit way, my clan name would come from my mother's side of the family?" Marissa asked.

"Yes, that's exactly right! You certainly are smart. You explained it much easier than I did," said Fran. She gave Marissa a gentle pat on the back.

Fran added, "Grandpa Kelly and Grandma Betty are actually my aunt and uncle. But in our Indian ways, we call all of our elders either Grandma or Grandpa, as a sign of respect. Marissa, I'm sure they would love to hear you call them that, too."

Marissa and Fran were getting closer to the top of the hill. They could smell the spruce, hemlock, and fir trees and the sweet-scented wildflowers that grew all over the hill. They stopped and looked toward the ocean. The village at the edge of the ocean spread out below them. A large pier pointed out into the bay, toward other evergreen-covered islands. Marissa felt the cool breeze blowing. She could hear birds moving from branch to branch in the trees behind her.

It was so pretty in Kake that Marissa didn't know what she liked best. She loved looking down on the village from up here. It seemed like she could see clouds a thousand miles away. She liked looking at the old wooden houses lined up along the shore with the beach as their backyard. They looked tiny from up here. But Marissa also liked to be at the ocean's edge, where she could look for creatures in the tide pools.

During her visit, Marissa spent some time exploring the shores of Kake. She especially enjoyed skimming rocks and looking for little sea creatures.

The day Marissa had arrived in Kake, her cousins had asked her if she wanted to go looking in the tide pools. Together, they found small starfish, baby crabs, mussels, and all sorts of other tiny ocean creatures. Marissa liked the pools so much that later on she returned by herself and found a creature that looked like a ball of overlapping shells. When she took it back to the house, Aunt Bambi told her it was a shellfish that people in Kake call a "gumboot."

"Marissa, what are you thinking about?" asked Fran as she stroked her granddaughter's long black hair.

"I was wondering if Kake always looked like this, Grandma," Marissa said.

"Well, there are a lot of things I haven't told you yet. Do you see how the houses down by the shore have their backs to the ocean? They're about 70 years old. You might think they are old, but there were even older houses here before these. My grandmother used to tell me how the Tlingits lived before I was born. That was when the Tlingit people lived in big clan houses made from huge planks of fir or spruce," said Fran. "Each clan house had several families living in it. These houses faced the ocean, and each one had a totem pole in front of it. Next to the totem poles, on the beach, there were also several big dugout canoes."

"Why did they have so many canoes?" asked Marissa.

"Back in those days, no one had cars, so people traveled mostly by canoe," Fran explained.

"Several men would take a dugout canoe to the ocean to fish for halibut or hunt for seal. Women and children would walk along the beach at low tide and dig for clams. When cars were invented and people started using them to get around the island, roads were built behind the clan houses. Later, new houses were built facing the road instead of the ocean. Of course, they still had to use canoes to get from island to island," Fran said.

After slowly walking up the hill, Marissa and Fran were finally approaching the totem pole. Marissa couldn't wait to learn about the giant monument that stood in front of her.

"This totem pole is one of the tallest in the world. It was built in 1971 and is over 132 feet tall," said Fran. "It was originally built for an international exposition in Japan. That's like a world's fair. But the totem pole was so large that it could not fit onto the ship. The totem pole had to be cut in half."

Fran continued, "After it was brought back from Japan, my father helped put it back together with a totem-raising crew. He was a boatbuilder and wood-carver. He was your great-grandfather, Marissa. His name was Paul Nannauck."

Marissa looked up at the totem pole. It was covered with designs that she recognized, such as Eagle and Raven, Killer Whale and Frog, Salmon and Bear.

"Grandma Fran, I always liked the designs on totem poles, but I never knew what a totem pole was for. I think I know now. Is it sort of a story about a family?" asked Marissa.

"That's right," Fran said. "A totem pole tells a family's history—something a group of people can respect and be proud of. When clan houses were around, the totem poles that families had in their front yards told other families about the history of the clan. Houses usually had more than one totem pole because when people got married, several clans lived in the same house."

Fran continued, "Some totem poles told about a particular family member's accomplishments. Other totem poles were used to keep the ashes of people who died and were cremated. Back then, Tlingits cremated the body of a loved one instead of burying it. A hole was carved in the back of the totem pole and then sealed after the person's ashes were put into it. Some clans built little houses at the base of a totem pole. These little houses were also used to keep the ashes of the family's ancestors."

"Grandma Fran, how come there aren't any other totem poles around?" asked Marissa. "What happened to all the totem poles you were talking about?"

"When the missionaries came here, they didn't understand that we used the totem poles as a type of family crest or emblem. The missionaries thought the people were worshipping the dead. They made the Kake Indians destroy their totem poles and move the remains of their people to Grave Island," Fran said. "That's the island over there. It is the cemetery where everyone is buried." She pointed to an island in the distance.

Then Fran and Marissa sat down by the totem pole. Fran said, "I noticed you were playing by the shore a few evenings ago, Marissa. What were you doing?"

"I was looking at all the tiny sea animals that live in the ocean. I was amazed at all the things I saw. I found a creature called a gumboot," Marissa said.

"The old Tlingit name for it is *shaoh* (SHAOW)—the same sound as in 'shower,'" said Grandma Fran. "I am really proud of you, Marissa. You're learning to be watchful and learn from nature—that is the Tlingit way of thinking. Our people have always been thankful to Mother Earth for all her gifts. We respect animals and plants because they have something to give us," she said.

"In the old days, people used all parts of an animal. Nothing was wasted. When I was your age, my mother taught me how to sew using sinew, which is a tendon from an animal. We used sinew from a deer, because it's usually the strongest. We made leather out of deer hides and sealskins. We made moccasins from the soft leather."

Fran continued, "We were also taught that things wouldn't come our way without a purpose. Once my Grandma Lizzie found a bit of copper somewhere. It wasn't to be wasted either. She used it to scrape out the inside of animal skins until they were soft."

Grandma Fran suggested that she and Marissa walk through the village of Kake. Before they started, they looked down at the village again. Fran said, "You were asking if Kake always looked this way. I told you about the days before I was born. The clan houses were still up then. But in 1926, only six years before I was born, a big fire in Kake burned everything down. It was a very sad time for everyone. People rebuilt their houses over the next two years, but it was a hard time. Some of the clan houses were never replaced."

Marissa had once seen a television program where a family lost its house in a fire. But she couldn't imagine what it would be like to see her whole town burn down. It must have been really awful, she thought.

Fran and Marissa walked back down the hill slowly. They watched the clouds move over the channel. The clear morning light had shifted into an afternoon glow. Near the path, they saw some children throwing down their fishing lines from a bridge over a creek. Marissa wondered what they were trying to catch.

"It looks like some kids are jigging for salmon," Fran said.

"What does the word 'jigging' mean, Grandma?" asked Marisssa.

"Do you see how the kids are moving their fishing lines with a jerky motion?" replied Fran. "That's called jigging." Marissa smiled and nodded.

When they got close enough to the creek, Marissa could see that it was boiling with activity. Marissa could not believe her eyes. The creek was entirely full of salmon! They swarmed over each other, tossing flecks of water that caught the sunlight.

As a boy showed them a big salmon he had just caught, a girl pointed far up the creek toward the forest. Fran looked toward the area where the girl was pointing.

"We have to be careful," Fran said. "There is a bear up the creek. Look, Marissa, have you ever seen a bear in the wild before? You can barely see it."

Marissa followed her grandmother's finger to a dark spot at the edge of the trees. Marissa was very excited. She had never seen a wild bear before. The dark spot was far away, but she could see that it was a big black bear. It was too busy eating salmon to notice it was being watched. The bear was having a feast!

Fran said, "This is one of the things we are most grateful for. The salmon runs are a special thing the Creator has provided for the Tlingit people. Each summer, the salmon come up the creeks from the ocean to lay their eggs in freshwater—it's called spawning. When the eggs hatch, the young fish swim back to the ocean, where they grow into adults. They come back to freshwater when they are ready to spawn, just as their parents did. It is a mystery how the fish return each year to the place of their birth."

Fran pointed to a large fish with black and green stripes. It was swimming close to the creek's edge. "These are dog salmon," she said. "When they're growing up in the ocean, they are one solid color, a silvery gray. They have stripes now that they are in freshwater. Their bodies change as the water changes. The other four kinds of salmon are king, sockeye, silver, and humpback. Dog salmon come back to the creeks here in Kake. The others go back to another island or to the mainland."

Fran continued, "People used to rely more on the ocean for their food. They still do, but these days, people go out in motorized boats instead of dugout canoes. When I was a young girl, we would all go to the summer fishing camps when the salmon came back to spawn. I loved to see the salmon fill up the rivers and creeks. The men would fish with nets or traps to catch the salmon. They would work together to bring the food home. Then the women would cut the salmon in strips and hang them in the smokehouse to dry.

"Let's walk over to see your Auntie Rosie. You met her at the family reunion. She said she might be smoking some salmon today," Fran said.

The family's smokehouse is used to smoke salmon during the summer months.

Auntie Rosie is Fran's sister. She lives in Kake. The smokehouse is right behind her house. Sometimes other family members, like Fran and her brother, Leonard, use the smokehouse, too.

Auntie Rosie's house is right on the edge of the water. Fran told Marissa that Auntie Rosie often complains about the bears that break into her smokehouse. She says that they are so lazy, they don't even catch their own fish.

When Fran and Marissa got to Auntie Rosie's house, she was already in the smokehouse. "Hi, Auntie Rosie, remember me?" Marissa called out. She and Grandma Fran both stepped into the smokehouse.

Auntie Rosie said, "Sure, I remember you, Marissa. I see your grandma has brought you over to learn about smoking salmon." Auntie Rosie had already cleaned the salmon and cut each one into thin strips. The strips hung off racks along the ceiling.

"The first thing you have to learn is to be very careful about how hot the fire is in the smokehouse," she said. "If the temperature is too high, the salmon will be dry and hard. You want the fish to be dry but still very tender. The trick is to keep the smokehouse the same mild temperature for several days. These strips are just about perfect."

Marissa had eaten smoked salmon before, but she had never seen how it was made. She liked the delicate taste. After their short visit, Fran and Marissa said good-bye to Auntie Rosie. Then they stepped outside and started walking back to Grandma Fran's house.

Auntie Rosie smokes salmon for three to five days, turning them every two to three hours, to make sure they'll be perfect.

Fran said, "Remember how I told you that Tlingit people never waste any part of an animal? It's the same for salmon. Tomorrow you can have some salmon eggs. They're a real delicacy. And remember I mentioned using sealskins for making moccasins? We also eat the seal meat. Usually we have lots of Tlingit foods at traditional celebrations. We had seal meat at the last potlatch."

Marissa remembered eating some seal meat at the family reunion. It tasted really good, sort of like bacon and sort of like fish, with a lingering sweet taste.

Marissa asked, "Grandma Fran, what are potlatches? I've heard people talk about them, but I don't really know what they are."

"A potlatch is a big celebration that Tlingit people have, usually in the winter. A particular family or clan holds a pot-latch to celebrate a fortunate event. Some people have a potlatch for a special occasion, like the raising of a new totem pole," said Fran.

"The head of a family or a designated clan leader usually decides when it is time to have a potlatch. For many months before the potlatch, the family remembers all the special things that other people in the village like. For instance, the wife of the clan leader might remember that her friend has admired one of her bone or ivory bracelets. She would have another made just like it. During the potlatch, the family members give presents to all the people there. Then they give special gifts, like the bracelets, to special friends or other clan leaders in the village."

"It sounds cool," Marissa said. "What else happens at a potlatch?"

"Well, a potlatch is usually filled with singing and dancing and feasting. Relatives who have died are remembered, and children are named. Sometimes, weddings are announced during a potlatch," said Fran.

She continued, "I remember the first potlatch I went to as a young girl. It was exciting, but I didn't understand all the traditions and what each one meant. The Tlingit songs sounded strange to me then, but now I know each one has its own special meaning. A potlatch, like the family reunion, is a time for families to celebrate their good fortune and give thanks for it."

Marissa was getting tired as she and Fran headed back to the house, but Marissa had many things on her mind. She was happy that she and her grandmother had gone for a walk. Marissa felt she understood her history and herself a little more.

When Marissa and Fran finally got back to the old family house, Fran gave Marissa an old photograph taken in 1955—it showed five generations of women in their family. The two oldest were Grandma Fran's Grandma Lizzie and Great-Grandmother Alice. Alice had lived back in the days when the only white people in Kake were missionaries and teachers. She used to joke that only preachers, teachers, and shopkeepers were brave enough to be around the Kake Indians.

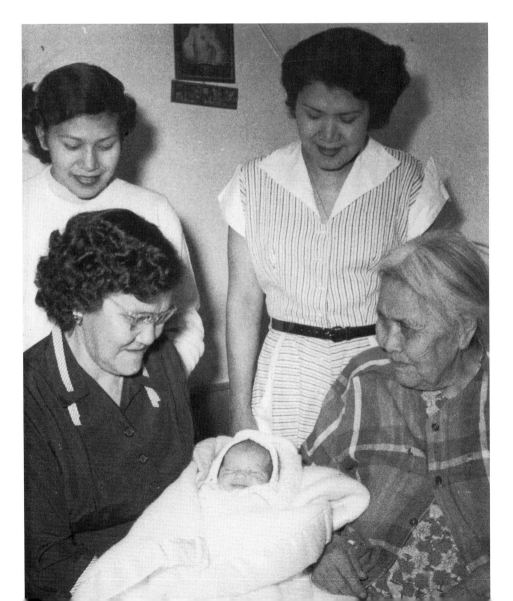

Clockwise from top left: *Frances Nannauck Kraus; Fran's mother, Charlotte (Lottie) Jackson Nannauck; Fran's great-grandmother, Alice Stuteen; Fran's eldest daughter, Debra Kraus; and Fran's grandmother, Elizabeth (Lizzie) Jackson*

"I told you how a clan name goes through a person's mother," Fran said. "I want you to know that you come from a family of very strong women. We have lots of stories to tell about our family."

"What do you mean by *strong*?" Marissa asked.

Fran replied, "Our people of Kake have gone through many hardships, but we have survived. We come from a family that is well respected for that reason. We are strong."

Marissa looked again at the photograph. It looked very old. Marissa thought about everything she had learned and about what it meant to be part of the Eagle people. Grandma Fran remembered a lot of things about her history—she must have learned those things from her Grandma Lizzie and Great-Grandma Alice, Marissa thought. Then she smiled and said, "Now I have a story to tell."

Word List

clan—a group of families descended from a common ancestor

clan house—a house that several related families live in together

dugout canoe—a boat made by hollowing out one side of a log

glacier (GLAY-shur)—a large body of ice usually found in mountain valleys

jigging—to move a fishing tool with a jerky motion, in order to catch fish

Kake (KUH-ck)—a village in southeastern Alaska; one of the homelands of the Tlingit Indians

missionaries (MISH-uh-nair-ees)—people from a church or a religious group who try to convert others to their faith

potlatch—a ceremony that celebrates a significant occasion such as a death, birth, or marriage; involves an abundance of food and presents

raven—a large black bird from the crow family

shaoh (SHAOW)—The old Tlingit word for a shellfish that looks like a ball of overlapping shells; people who live in Kake call it a *gumboot*. The English word for it is "chiton."

sinew (SIN-yoo)—a strong band of tissue (usually a tendon) from an animal; sometimes used as a cord or thread

smokehouse—a building where fish or meat is smoked and dried

spawn—to lay and fertilize a large number of eggs

tide pool—a small sand pool formed by the continual movement of waves along a shore

Tlingit (KLINK-it)—Indian people who live mostly in the southeastern part of Alaska. Tlingit means "the People."

totem pole—a pole, usually made of wood, that is carved with animals and other natural objects to illustrate a family's history

For Further Reading

Cheney, Cora. *Alaska: Indians, Eskimos, Russians and the Rest.* New York: Dodd, Mead & Company, 1980.

Johnston, Joyce. *Alaska.* Minneapolis: Lerner Publications Company, 1997.

Mercredi, Morningstar. *Fort Chipewyan Homecoming.* Minneapolis: Lerner Publications Company, 1997.

Murphy, Claire Rudolf. *A Child's Alaska.* Anchorage: Alaska Northwest Books, 1994.

Osinski, Alice. *The Tlingit.* Chicago: Childrens Press, 1990.

We Are Still Here: Native Americans Today

Children of Clay: *A Family of Pueblo Potters*

Clambake: *A Wampanoag Tradition*

Drumbeat...Heartbeat: *A Celebration of the Powwow*

Fort Chipewyan Homecoming: *A Journey to Native Canada*

Four Seasons of Corn: *A Winnebago Tradition*

Ininatig's Gift of Sugar: *Traditional Native Sugarmaking*

Kinaaldá: *A Navajo Girl Grows Up*

The Sacred Harvest: *Ojibway Wild Rice Gathering*

Shannon: *An Ojibway Dancer*

Songs from the Loom: *A Navajo Girl Learns to Weave*

A Story to Tell: *Traditions of a Tlingit Community*

Weaving a California Tradition: *A Native American Basketmaker*

About the Contributors

Richard Nichols is a Tewa Pueblo educator and writer from the Santa Clara Indian Pueblo in New Mexico. He has served as a curriculum consultant with Harcourt Brace on its social studies textbook series, and with Reader's Digest on its book *Through Indian Eyes: The Untold Story of Native American Peoples.* Since 1982, Richard has been vice president of ORBIS Associates, an Indian-controlled, Indian-managed educational research and management consulting organization in Washington, D.C. Fluent in his native language, Richard is a member of the Summer People of his tribe. He lives in Washington, D.C.

D. Bambi Kraus was born and raised in Seattle, Washington, and graduated from Stanford University with a B.A. degree in Anthropology. She resides in Washington, D.C., where she has held a variety of positions regarding national Indian policy issues. She has also worked, and continues to work, as a freelance photographer. In 1994, she won the "Best of Division" for color photography at the Indian Market Photography Exhibit in Santa Fe, New Mexico. Bambi currently serves as an elected board member of the 13th Regional Corporation, an Alaska Native for-profit corporation that was created by the Alaska Native Claims Settlement Act.

Series Editor **Gordon Regguinti** is a member of the Leech Lake Band of Ojibway. He was raised on Leech Lake Reservation in Minnesota by his mother and grandparents. His Ojibway heritage has remained a central focus of his professional life. A graduate of the University of Minnesota with a B.A. degree in Indian Studies, Regguinti has written about Native American issues for newspapers and school curricula. He served as the editor of a Minneapolis–St. Paul Native American newspaper *The Circle* for two years and as the executive director of the Native American Journalists Association. He lives in Minneapolis and has six children and four grandchildren.

Series Consultant **W. Roger Buffalohead** is a member of the Ponca Tribe in Oklahoma. He has been involved in Indian education for more than 20 years, serving as a national consultant to Indian education programs, Indian media projects, and museum programs. Buffalohead has an M.A. degree in American History from the University of Wisconsin, Madison. He has taught at the University of Cincinnati, the University of California, Los Angeles, and the University of Minnesota, where he was the acting chair of the department of American Indian Studies and later the director of the American Indian Learning and Resources Center. Recently, Buffalohead served as the acting dean of the Center for Arts and Cultural Studies at the Institute of American Indian Arts in Santa Fe. Currently, he is a freelance consultant and lives in Minneapolis.

Illustrator **Carly Bordeau** is a member of the Anishinabe Nation, White Earth, Minnesota. She graduated from the College of Associated Arts in St. Paul with a B.A. degree in Graphic Design. Carly is the owner of All Nite Design and Photography, and she enjoys freelancing as a graphic designer, illustrator, and photographer. She lives in St. Paul.